CORNERSTONES AND KEYSTONES

SOLID FOUNDATIONS FOR SUCCESS IN BUSINESS AND LIFE

CORNERSTONES AND KEYSTONES

SOLID FOUNDATIONS FOR SUCCESS IN BUSINESS AND LIFE

The statements, opinions, and data contained in this publication are solely those of the author of each individual chapter and not of the publisher, the editor, or other authors.

No express or implied guarantees or warranties have been made or are made by the author or publisher regarding outcomes. Neither author nor publisher accepts any liability or responsibility to any person or entity with respect to any loss or damage alleged to have been caused, directly or indirectly, by the information, ideas, opinions or other content in this book.

All rights reserved. No part of this publication may be reproduced, distributed, or transmitted in any form or by any means, including photocopying, recording, or other electronic or mechanical methods, without the prior written permission of the publisher, except in the case of brief quotations embodied in critical reviews and certain other noncommercial uses permitted by copyright law.

For permission requests, contact the publisher at
sales@canlead.ca.

Ordering Information:
Quantity sales. Special discounts are available for bulk purchases by corporations, associations, and others. For details, contact the publisher at the address above.

Printed in the United States of America
ISBN: 978-0-9940519-5-0
First Edition
14 13 12 11 10 / 10 9 8 7 6 5 4 3 2

Contents

Kathy's Story: A Story about Change	7
By **Michael Bayer**	
About the Author	17
Take Control of Your Life	19
By **Emma Frost**	
About the Author	27
Exploring Your Potential and Achieving Success	29
By **Man Doan**	
About the Author	39
It's All about People; A Journey of Discovery	41
By **Karen Kaplen**	
About the Author	47
Rules of Engagement for Adult Conversation	49
By **Catherine Kellar**	
About the Author	61
Executives and IT – On the Same Page	63
By **Kurt Penner**	
About the Author	73
Laverne's Life Lessons from the Pumpkin Patch	75
By **Laverne Wojciechowski**	
About the Author	87
Discover the Magic of Believing in You	89
By **Greg Wood**	
About the Author	103
Finding Your Passion through Service	105
By **David Woodcock**	
About the Author	115

Contact Information

Kathy's Story: A Story About Change
by Michael Bayer

Many years ago, I was the supervisor of telecommunications at Transport Canada. I worked with engineers and telecommunications officers managing the voice and data networks. Kathy was part of our team. She was our unit clerk who paid the bills, made travel arrangements, and generally kept us all in-line. Part of her job description was to fill in for the telecommunications officer, who reported to me, whenever they were on leave. She always said the telecommunications officer's job was going to be hers one day. However, whenever there was an opportunity to put her in the job to fill in for vacation or other leaves, she would refuse, and we had to recruit someone else to fill-in. This was an onerous task because it involved a lot of what turned out to be one-time training as we could never get the same person back. It was not an optimal solution.

Jackie, my telecommunications officer, approached me one day and asked me if she could take a three-month assignment working on a special project in another government department. I agree to let her go, but that meant that I had a problem; I needed to back-fill the telecommunications officer position for three months.

I felt that this was the time to take the bull by the horns. I spoke with Ken, our boss and told him that I wanted to put Kathy in the job and recruit a clerk to fill in. Filling in a clerical position was much simpler than filling in a technical position. I explained that if we did this, in the future, we wouldn't be faced with the problem if someone went on vacation. We would have the trained staff in our unit to be able to fill-in immediately. It was relatively easy to recruit a unit clerk. He said okay but be careful and warned me that I was going to run into some resistance.

There is a misconception that people are resistant to change and that this resistance to change is a key factor in the difficulty of initiating change within organizations. I believe this is a myth. I feel that the biggest challenge we have is not resistance to change but rather the resistance that we have to being changed.

In order to examine this further, let's examine the three distinct phases of change.

The first phase is the decision to change. This is the most difficult phase of the change process. Once the individual has weighed the pros and cons and realizes the necessity that change is required, they make the decision to change.

A prime example is the smartphone, a device that virtually every one of us has in their pocket, purse or briefcase. This electronic device has become pervasive in our lives since it was introduced only ten years ago. In one simple small device, we can surf the web, take pictures, take videos, read newspapers, organize our time, get emails and do a variety of other functions that ten years ago we would have never even imagined on such a small device.

So why is this device found in virtually everyone's hand today? The manufacturers of these devices have shown us how we can simplify our lives by integrating all of these functions into one small handheld device. When we look back and think about the different devices and things we had to carry in the past, in order to accomplish what this one small device can today, we realize that has its benefits. So, we have adopted the smartphone as part of our daily lives. We weren't resistant to change away from using the other devices because we saw the advantage of having all the devices in one simple small package that does things better than all the old devices did put together. This process of accepting a new device is the first phase of change. The role of a manager is to help individuals past their resistance to change. When we can show them the advantages of the change, in terms of the benefits to them, they embrace the change.

The second phase of change is the transition phase. This is the most exciting phase of the process as it involves experimentation, innovation, and change. There are no guiding principles. There is no established policy or procedural guidelines. The only principle is: Are we doing the right thing to further our mission, vision, and values? If the answer is yes, we continue, looking for 1% improvement if possible and constantly try to innovate change. If the answer is no, we see if we can improve it or change it. If we can, we make the change. If not, we discard the idea and try something else.

A problem can occur during the transition phase of change. If people are suddenly empowered to make a change as they see fit in accordance with the new guidelines, they may not rise to the occasion for fear of making mistakes. This could seriously stifle creativity during the transition phase of change.

Empowerment can sometimes be defined as the gift of adulthood. Not everyone is ready to receive this gift. As managers, we have to manage people through the transition phase of change carefully. Not everyone readily embraces empowerment. An effective way of managing this transition is to empower people as their self-confidence increases gradually. This can also help the manager feel more comfortable knowing that the individuals are growing into their roles.

This process has a number of levels.

The first level is delegation. The individual looks into the problem reports the facts and then brings them back to the manager. The manager will decide.

The second level is pre-empowerment. Once the individual has the facts, knows what the alternative actions are, has weighed the pros and cons and recommended an action, the manager will decide.

The third level is conditional empowerment. Take all the previous steps, let the manager know what you intend to do but don't take any action until it's been approved.

The fourth level is semi-empowerment. Let the manager know what you intend to do and do it unless the manager says no.

The last level is full empowerment. Take the appropriate action, no contact with the manager is necessary unless you feel it is necessary.

Working through the steps with someone is a very powerful way of gradually empowering them. It boosts their self-confidence. It also gives you a sense of control in that you're aware of what they're doing and that they are comfortable in their new role.

I met with Kathy and explained what we wanted to do. She was not happy. I explained advantages to her career and advancement potential. I explained how this would benefit not only our department but the technical services branch as well. She could see the advantages but was resisting. I asked why. She told me she had no idea about how to do that job.

I told her I would train her. I asked her to book a training room twice a week for two hours, and we would have Telecom school. We spent four weeks training. At the end of the four weeks, I felt Kathy was ready, with careful supervision, to take over the role of telecommunications officer.

The day finally came when Jackie left on her assignment, and Kathy took over her job. She was very nervous and unsure of herself. She said to me "I think I have made a mistake. I don't know if I can do this." The resistance to being changed was still there.

I realized that the best thing to do was walk through the five levels of empowerment and slowly delegate the responsibilities of the job to Kathy. I started out by assigning her work and asking her to gather the facts, bring them to me and I would make a decision. After a short while, I started asking her for a recommendation as to the course of action. We would talk about her recommendations, weigh the pros and cons and then make a decision on whether or not that was the course of action we would take. Kathy developed a solid grasp of the needs of our customers, the solutions to their problems and the course of action we needed to take to solve their problems. We would go to the point where I said "Do the analysis, write up the order and bring it to me for approval before you send it." Eventually, we got to the point where she was assigned work, and she just processed the orders. I would, of course, check her work from time to time because I was ultimately responsible.

Kathy thrived in the environment we had created. As her responsibilities grew, so did her self-confidence. Eventually the day she dreaded of arrived. Jackie was back to work, and she went back to her regular job.

Two months later, our world changed again. Jackie announced she had accepted a job in another department and she was leaving. This created a vacancy we needed to fill. Ken and I talked about appointing her but decided we would run a real competition. We posted the job and received 92 applications. Kathy's was one of them.

There was a problem with her qualifications. The position required a driver's licence. Kathy didn't know how to drive. She managed her life with public transit or taxis. I called her into my office and told her if she didn't have a valid driver's licence when we offered the job, she would be screened out.

She took the news quietly.

Several weeks later I was out of town on a business trip where everything seemed to go wrong. It was late Friday; I had just changed my reservations for the next day, needing to spend an extra night on the road when I decided I should perhaps check in with the office. Kathy answered the phone with a "Where have you been all day and why haven't you checked in earlier" greeting. She was bubbling with excitement. That morning she had passed her driving test!

Two weeks later, after a series of interviews, there was only one person left standing, and she stood tall. We offered, and she accepted the job that started her down a career path she had only dreamed of before.

On Sept 28, 1997, our world changed again in a way we never expected. At a full mandatory staff meeting, we were told the operation was being shut down, 13 jobs would transfer out, and the rest of us would be laid off. We were stunned. It started the third phase of change, the new beginning.

As things unfolded, I was offered a transfer. My family did not want to move, so in an interview, I declined the position. I was told that my job was essential and asked who could do it. I said: "Kathy. She has earned it."

We all parted ways a few months later, me to a new and exciting career and Kathy, newly promoted, to new adventures in a new city ready to take on new challenges.

Kathy's story is a story about change. The first part of the story is about an individual who, because of necessity, accepted that being changed was in her best interest. The importance of open two-way communication in managing change cannot be overstated. You cannot over-communicate during change. You have to constantly tell people in terms of what they understand and in terms of benefits to them why the change needs to be done, how they will benefit because of the change, how they will grow because of the change and the impact on the organization if we don't change. We can never assume that our staff understands and sees the same big picture we do. Our role as manager in the change process is to help them see that in terms that they understand.

There are few sure things in life and business. Benjamin Franklin said the only two things in life we can be sure of are death and taxes. He forgot one. Change. The survival of our organizations depends on how well we manage change.

Is your organization undergoing rapid change?

How are you being forced to fundamentally change the way you do business in order to survive in today's environment? If you are facing change, you must constantly ask yourself how well am I managing this change? Do my people understand the need for the change? Do my people see the benefit to them individually as a result of this change? If we answer all of these questions yes, we will probably be very successful in managing the transition phase of change that leads to a new beginning.

If you answered no, perhaps you need the help of a professional to help guide your organization through the transition phase of change. How well you manage the transition phase of change will determine how well your organization survives.

About the Author

As President of The LEAN Consulting Group, Michael Bayer leads a highly-trained group of consultants skilled at implementing sustainable LEAN practices. He has an MBA and is a certified LEAN Black Belt for Healthcare.

His 12-year background as a senior telecommunications manager in government coupled with over 18 years at the forefront of initiatives in quality management at hospitals and healthcare organizations across the United States and Canada have solidified his reputation as a change agent.

Michael teaches organizations the living, breathing, essential LEAN processes that build successful, self-sustaining corporate cultures.

Michael Bayer
(204) 237-9257
Toll-Free: 1-888-551-5592
michael@theleanconsultinggroup.com

TAKE CONTROL OF YOUR LIFE
BY EMMA FROST

Taking Control of Your Life is all about doing what you want to do. It is all about realizing your dreams and turning them into achievable goals. It is about identifying what is missing from your life, and working out how to fill the gap. It is about turning your life around, being happy, and making a difference.

Sometimes life gets the better of us. We wonder why we are not enjoying ourselves anymore. We wonder "when did life stop being fun?" We ask ourselves "when did we lose control?" At times like this, most people fall back on blaming someone else, their parents, their boss, their spouse, their kids, anyone but themselves should take responsibility for them no longer enjoying their life. When I was eight years old, people used to ask me what I wanted to be when I was grown up. My answer was twenty-three. I chose twenty-three because I had worked out that when I was that old, no one could tell me what to do anymore. I would finally be in charge of my decisions. However, when I finally reached the age of twenty-three, I had forgotten about my dreams of living a free and easy life. I was working in a job I was not happy with, living in a flat I did not really like, with someone I would not have chosen to live with if I had known more about them when we decided to share a place. I was not even thinking about what I was going to be doing in the future. My life was just something that happened while I was busy doing something else. I had lost sight of my dreams.

I am here to tell you that you only get one go at this "life" thing. There is no rehearsal, where you can make mistakes, and go back and fix them. There is only your future. Moreover, you have to step up and take control of the rest of your time on earth. I am going to give you three ways to start taking back control.

1. Remember your childhood dreams

There are some very basic steps that you need to take to take back control. The first, and arguably the most important, is to remember the dreams you had when your imagination had no limits. Then remember why you had that dream. When I was dreaming of being twenty-three, it was not about the age; it was about the freedom I thought I would have to make my own decisions. Because I was only 8 when I wanted to live that dream, It was many years before I woke up and realized that I still wasn't living my life the way I had dreamed back then. I had allowed other people to make the most important decisions in my life. At that time, I walked away from a 32-year career doing something I really didn't like, with people I didn't really like. I had drifted into a holding pattern, letting my life drift by without anyone at the wheel. I finally took control and steered myself in the right direction. I sat down and thought about my dreams, thought about what it is that I want out of life, and how I could achieve that.

When I walked away from my research career, I knew it was a huge risk, but it was one I had to take. My passion is to help people live better lives, and to find their voice in the cacophony of sound that bombards us from all sides. I was not able to do this from a dark and dingy office, working for someone else, by another set of rules. I had to step out into the light and lead by example. I had to live my dream.

2. Develop achievable goals

Once you have remembered your idealistic life, you need to work out how to make it real. The first step is to turn those dreams into goals that are achievable. When you are thinking about this, I want you to know that nothing is impossible. I met an eighty-two-year-old gentleman recently who wanted to be an astronaut when he was a young boy. When I told him that he could still go into space to experience what the world looked like from above, he laughed. However, when I described the steps he would need to take to achieve his goal, his expression changed to wonder, then to one of excitement. I had made his boyhood dreams a potentially achievable goal, and for the first time in his life, he felt as though he actually could go out into space.

No matter how crazy your dreams were, you can make them a reality by thinking through, step by step, what it is you need to do to succeed. Sometimes the steps might seem too high to climb. In that case, simply break them down into smaller steps. Just like eating an elephant. You will only succeed if you take a single bite at a time.

3. Organize your time

Many people bemoan the lack of time to get things done. In reality, they just need to be better organized. By learning how to waste less time on meaningless activities, you can increase the amount of time you have to realize your dreams. There are many ways that you can make better use of your day. Probably the easiest way is to keep track of everything that you do every day for a week. Then go back and add up all the minutes you spent on each separate activity. Finally, decide which activities will help you to achieve your goal. Once you know where you are spending your minutes, you can work out how to make better use of those minutes to achieve your goals.

I had a client a few years ago, who had an extremely demanding job. She was in charge of two departments within her organization. She had two offices, in separate parts of the building, with two different groups of staff to lead. Each office had its own culture and working vibe. My client was frenetically running from office to office trying to stay on top of her workload. When she looked at where she was spending her workday minutes, it was evident that she was spending too much time running between offices. She changed her processes so that she spent the first four hours of the day in one office, and the last four hours of the day in the other.

She alternated morning and afternoon "shifts," and made sure that her assistant in each office always knew where she was. Her life became much less harried. Also, she found that she was spending 45-60 minutes a day getting coffee. When she added up how long it took to get to the Starbucks on the ground floor of her building, wait in line for her caramel macchiato, and then get back again, twice a day, she was horrified. She installed a coffee machine in her offices, bought coffee and cream, made them available to her teams, and saved herself nearly an hour a day.

4. Grow confident in your decision making

Fear of failure is an insurmountable barrier for many people. The fear can come from many sources. Sometimes it develops from a decision made in childhood that went horribly wrong. Sometimes it originates from a fear of not achieving perfection. Sometimes it develops from a lack of practice at making decisions or needing to have decisions approved. Whatever the source of the blockage, it is possible to overcome the fear and achieve success.

Every day we make decisions without even realizing it. When the alarm goes off, we make the decision to get out of bed. We make the decision to have breakfast, to shower, to clean our teeth. When we bought the coffee, we made a decision about which brand to buy, which store to shop in, and how to grind the beans. We chose the toothpaste, the soap, and the shampoo. These are decisions that we make without much thought or planning, and with no worry about what will happen if we get it wrong. When you have to make a life-changing decision a whole bundle of insecurities and fears jumps into view and blocks your path forward. The trick is learning how to see around those barriers and recognizing that not making the decision leaves you worse off.

Making a decision can be accomplished by working through a few simple steps, based on an understanding of what it is you are trying to achieve. The first, most important step, is to gather information relating to your decision. You need to know as much about the subject as possible, both positive and negative. The second phase is to take all that information and interpret it. You need to weigh the benefits and consequences of each alternative in the decision. The final step is to make the decision and act upon it.

Sometimes our gut takes over, and we just go with it. Like when, as a child, you decide to try to jump across the stream. You do not spend any time thinking about it; you do not consider the consequences or even the different outcomes. You just jump. Then, when you get home covered in mud and soaking wet, and your mum asks you why you can correctly say "it seemed like the right thing to do at the time." As an adult, you return to the stream, and you see that the other bank is slippery with wet mud, steep, and too high to land on with your feet. You can very quickly judge the situation and know that there is a high risk of failure (in that you will not make it to the other bank). You might still go for it, just for fun, or you might decide that you are too old to be rolling around in the muddy water, and go home instead. Gut decisions we take as an adult rarely have catastrophic consequences. Although, I did once drive into a ditch when trying to do a U-turn, on a narrow country road, in deep snow. However, in my defense, we met a wonderful gentleman who taught us a lot about living a peaceful life, so there were benefits.

There are now studies that show relying on gut instinct, or hunches work well in a business environment where you already have an in-depth knowledge of the problem. Reflexive response is faster than thoughtful consideration and may result in better decision making. An example of this is Steve Jobs, and the iPad, his decision to go ahead with the handheld device went against all the data available. Richard Branson is another highly successful business leader who uses his gut to make decisions. It is noteworthy that relying on hunches is not recommended in relationship decision making.

There are many other ways you can take control of your life. Making changes in how you think and react to the people around you, and the places that you visit is another great way to achieve control. Learn to recognize negativity and move away from it. Negative people can be Debbie Downers even in the most fun environment. Avoid these people as much as you can, and start looking at life through a positive lens. When things go wrong, don't blame others first, look inwards to see if it is you that needs to change.

Take control of your life is my message — I will guide you through practical, easy and fun challenges to help you live the life you dreamed of, and Rule Your World!

About the Author

Emma Frost, Ph.D., best-selling author of *"The Quick and Easy Way to Take Control of Your Life,"* is a personal development coach. In 2012, Emma finally took control of her life and walked away from her 32-year career as a research neuroscientist. She shares her experience with others and helps them to Rule Their World.

She has been mentoring and training for over fifteen years; and helps people identify and develop their leadership skills so that they can think better, work better and live better. As a certified trainer with the International Board of Certified Trainers, Emma works with groups and individuals to help them find their fabulous!

Emma is an Emerald Member of the International Women's Leadership Association, a Manitoba Keystone Speaker and longtime member of Toastmasters International. In 2008 she competed in the semi-finals of the World Championship of Public Speaking.

Emma Frost
info@rulyourworld.ca

EXPLORING YOUR POTENTIAL AND ACHIEVING SUCCESS
BY MAN DOAN

Into every life, a little rain must fall. On Father's Day June 21, 2015, I ran into a heart attack. Over the next few months, I was slowly recovering to normal activities, physically and mentally. Although I seemed to feel physically normal, mentally I was doubting myself and my abilities to do all the things that I wanted to do in life. That's when I realized that I had been wasting a lot of time. I was stuck in a rut of my own world. I thought I had accomplished a lot in my standard but in reality, I was limiting my own potential.

We all have the seeds of greatness within us. But many people are not even aware that they are the ones who restrain themselves from unleashing their potential. Sometimes, you just have to be true to yourself, face the reality, make a commitment and find a way to get out of your rut. I was writing this chapter to hopefully help you turn a new chapter in your life. This is a story that changed my life forever.

In the mid-90s, I made the first biggest decision in my life that shaped who I am today. I left behind my family, my relatives, my friends, my comfortable life and surroundings in the pursuit of something new. Something else new and better that everybody seemed to agree, but it was very abstract to me. Nothing concrete, nothing real that I can touch or see. I came to Canada as an international student. I was one of the first few Vietnamese international students in Winnipeg, Manitoba back then. I was on a path of adventure to explore my potential.

Three days before I was coming to Canada, my Dad was diagnosed with leukemia. I rushed to the hospital. He was already in a coma. It was a little too late. We were all by his side. Feeling hopeless and desperate, my Mom told me: "Son, you have to study hard and become a doctor." I came to hug Mom, comforting her, crying on the inside, I said "Yes Mom."

Back in Vietnam, I was in a specialized high school program that prepares students to advance to medical school. It was very competitive. We all had a dream to become doctors. There was a bigger dream for the Vietnamese students to pursue an education in Western countries such as Canada and US. My parents had worked hard all their lives to provide for my brother and me. Even though I had a very comfortable life, was quite popular and had a lot of friends, I was somehow convinced that coming to Canada would give me more opportunities, a stable career, a bright future, a better life.

Before coming to Winnipeg, I barely knew anything about the city. There was no internet, no cell phones, and no social networks. Google wasn't even a word. The first few years in Canada were a very difficult time for me. It's the first time I had been away from home. Everything was so new and different from what I was used to. Back then, I was required to pass a TOEFL English exam and retake grade 12 before moving onto university. I also found out that because of my visa status, I was not allowed to enroll into medical school. I was lost and devastated. All my life, I was groomed to become a doctor. I was determined because I thought it was expected of me, by my family, by our culture. Now, I had no choice but to choose a different career path.

I did not know what else to do with my life. I went to an Adult Education Centre. My classmates were mostly mature adults. I felt so displaced and humiliated that I had to retake grade 12 while my friends back home were already in their second year of medical school. I started to doubt myself, doubt my decision to come to Winnipeg. I was constantly struggling with self-confidence. I felt helpless and shameful as I was not able to fulfill my parents' wish. I was worried about what people would think of me. School was okay, but I really struggled with the new life, adjusting to the new culture, the language barrier, the cold weather, and above all, grieving my father's death. I became withdrawn from the world.

In my first year at the University of Manitoba, I randomly picked an introduction course in each faculty. One of them was computer science 101. I didn't know anything about computer science before. I thought perhaps it would help me improve my typing skills, not just poking on the keyboard with two fingers. What started as a typing lesson, quickly turned into a wonderful journey into the world of computers and programming. My first computer program I wrote was the famous "Hello World!" In my second year, I became more passionate and fascinated with it. I developed my own version of a chess game. I designed my first personal website. I was also qualified to enter the co-op program, studying and working to support myself.

I had a lot of challenges in my career and life. Communication was not my strongest point. I was terrified of presentation and public speaking. But I realized that if I was going to do well with what I wanted to do, I needed to be able to get up in front of people and talk. I was so glad that my colleague Brian introduced me to Toastmasters International, a world leading organization in communication and leadership development. Toastmasters has helped me become a more competent speaker and effective leader. It has helped me grow personally and professionally. But most of all, Toastmasters has given me the confidence I needed to express myself, to realize my full potential and do what I want to do with my life.

Fast forward many years, now I have a Master of Science Degree in Information Systems. I love my career as an IT Director. Sometimes I can't help but wonder had I stayed in Vietnam, what direction my life would have taken me. Would I be a doctor or a dentist like most of my high school friends as we were groomed to be? Would I become a pop star as my younger self once wished? Or would I have lost myself with no sense of direction and purpose in life? I have no idea. But one thing I know is I have a beautiful family, and I have no regrets about the decision to come to Canada. I love what I do in my professional career. I also discovered my passion in public speaking, coaching people on professional and personal development, helping others reach their potential.

I realized the pressure that I felt all those years, was created by no one but me. I was focusing more on my friends' accomplishments instead of my own. I was struggling with confidence and doubting myself for nothing. I am grateful for all the love, support and guidance of my family and relatives both in Vietnam and Canada throughout the years. I'm so glad that I persevered and found the courage to be myself once again, to discover my true passion, to explore my own potential, and have the freedom to do what I really wanted to do in life.

Potential. I believe that each and every one of us has the potential to succeed and be great. Some people might have lots of it. Some people might be wasting theirs. It's not how much potential you have, but it's what you want to do with it that matters most. Only you may know what your true potential is. You have options, and you are in control of your own life. Sometimes, you may have to adjust your plans because of the environment or the circumstances. Exploring different options, overcoming barriers that limit your potential allows you to alter your fate, redefine your destiny and change your life.

In the spring of 2015, I decided to do something fun and challenging together with my family. We entered a team relay full marathon with Manitoba Marathon as the "House of Dragons": me, my wife, my two daughters and my youngest 8-year-old son, along with fifteen others of my extended family. We had never run a long distance before. Actually, we never ran, period. We started training about three months before the event. It was really challenging, but everyone would push through, encourage and motivate each other, trying to stick to the training schedule.

On race day, I ran the first leg for about 9km. My wife and daughter were getting ready to run their third leg. I finished and came home around 9 o'clock. I took a shower and started feeling something unusual in my body. I went out to the living room, sat down to watch TV and having some snacks. Thirty minutes later, I was feeling dizzy and nauseated. For some reason, I didn't want to be alone, so I went into the room with my son. I was lying down next to him while he was reading a book. For the next hour, the symptoms were getting worse and worse. I was having discomfort in the chest. The pain was in all my body, spreading from the chest to the neck, shoulder, arms and back. It was burning, squeezing and becoming heavier and tighter with every breath I take.

I wanted to call my wife and daughters, but I did not want to interrupt their runs. The longer I waited, the more I was feeling uncomfortable and having a mixed emotion of fear, anxiety, denial and pain all at the same time. I was having cold sweats. My skin became pale, cool and damp. I had never experienced this before. My instinct told me this is something very serious, but I was in denial that I did not need medical attention and that it would get better soon. Then suddenly, an electric shock pain shot through my chest. It felt like an elephant stomping on my chest. I couldn't breathe. I really thought that I was going to die. I was gasping for air then passed out. And that's when I saw the light. My whole life flashed before my eyes, just like a movie. I saw myself as a young boy growing up in Vietnam then coming to Canada as a visa student. I met my wife in school, got married and had children. When I opened my eyes, I saw my wife and daughters. They had come home just in time. I was rushed to the hospital and diagnosed with a myocardial infarction, a heart attack. They found a 99.7% blockage in my artery. It could have been worse. I could have been dead.

I exercise regularly and have been physically active most of my life. I never had any heart diseases or problems. I believe the incident was merely a freak accident. Ironically, the heart attack was one of the best things that ever happened to me. It was a Father's Day gift that I never ever expected. And it was truly the most meaningful gift I have ever received, the gift of appreciation. Appreciation for life and for all the little things that sometimes we take for granted.

I believe that you must put yourself first when it

comes to health. You have to take care of your health because if you don't, no one else can do it for you. When you are healthy, you can take care of your family and love ones. When you are healthy, your mind and spirit will lift up. When you are healthy, you will have the energy to explore and achieve your potential. It's amazing how you can feel you are in control and can accomplish anything you set out to do.

One of the things that I love doing now is training for and running a marathon. I never thought that I would love this kind of sport. I have to attribute this to my cousin Yenny for starting this wonderful "House of Dragons" family running tradition that got us all closer through hard work, support and fun family bonding get-togethers. Not long before, I was barely able to run more than one mile. My kids, my cousins, and my work colleagues are my inspiration to help me keep on running. They showed me no matter what challenges you may have, if you persevere and focus, you can accomplish anything.

Now I am determined more than ever to one day run a full marathon and cross it off my bucket list. To achieve it, I have to divide and conquer, break it down into smaller steps. I have to set SMART goals; goals that are Specific, Measurable, Ambitious, Realistic with a Time-bound element. I started training six months after the heart attack with the approval of my cardiologist. I came back and ran a 10K event the following year. Then I wanted to up my game and set my target next on a half marathon (13.1 miles or 21.1 kilometers). I have been training five days a week and was able to achieve a significant milestone that I set for myself. I ran the half marathon at an indoor running track, all by myself, over two and a half hours of perseverance, determination, and dedication. It was an unforgettable journey of self-discovery. The feeling of satisfaction, accomplishment, and success is just amazing. My next milestone is to run the half marathon officially for the first time at the Manitoba Marathon on Father's Day June 18, 2017, two years after my heart attack. After that, I am going to train and continue to run three to five half marathon events before attempting my first full marathon within five years.

I am grateful for all the love and support of the people in my life. I came back from the heart attack stronger than ever, physically and mentally. The whole experience somehow helped me in exploring a new world of potential that I thought I never had. I made a commitment to stop wasting my time on meaningless things. I found a way to climb the walls and get myself of my own rut. I have more time to do more meaningful activities, enjoy life and be happy.

You don't need to go through a life changing event to realize that you should never stop growing. Whether it's about your health, career or self-development, you should always be looking to learn and grow, maximize your potential, increase your capacity and enjoyment of life. I was writing this chapter to help you explore your potential. Ironically, I was just starting to fulfill my own potential. Here are the five steps you can take to overcome fears, get out of any rut, clear your doubts, build your confidence, unleash your potential:

1. Make a decision and commitment to grow.
2. Set SMART goals and do it.
3. Divide and conquer, take smaller steps.
4. Celebrate your milestones and success, big or small.
5. Repeat.

Success is living up to your potential. Go ahead and fulfill yours!

About the Author

Man Doan works with organizations to improve operational efficiency and effectiveness, increase employee engagement and productivity, enhance customer satisfaction and increase financial performance.

Man has over 17 years of knowledge and experience in Information and Communications Technology including IT governance and management, strategic planning, Lean process improvement, business analysis, systems development, organizational change and project management.

Man has held many executive and leadership positions. As a member of a Manitoba premier Speakers Bureau, Man delivers keynotes, holds technical workshops and speaks on professional and personal development topics.

Man holds a Masters Degree in Information Systems, a BSc in Computer Science, and Certificates in Business Analysis, Project Management, Lean Management and Organizational Change Management.

Man Doan
man@mandoan.com
www.ManDoan.com

IT'S ALL ABOUT PEOPLE
A JOURNEY OF DISCOVERY
BY KAREN KAPLEN

This chapter is about my journey of self-discovery and finding my passion in life. It tells about how instilling hope can lead towards recovery and how this can benefit you and your bottom line.

I have had experience in many fields of business over the years including working as an office clerk, a sales person, a receptionist and a secretary. However, it wasn't until I started working with people living with a mental illness that I discovered my true passion in life. After working as a secretary for the Manitoba Schizophrenia Society (MSS) for seven years, I was offered the position of Women's Program Coordinator for the organization. This entailed taking an Applied Counselling Skills course at Red River Community College and working with two other facilitators as I learned how to conduct groups and provide one-on-one consultations with group members.

The Women's Program was started after Dr. Diana Clark, from the University of Manitoba Schizophrenia Treatment Education Program at the

Health Science Centre in Winnipeg, with Dr. Wanda Chernomas, from the Faculty of Nursing at the University of Manitoba and Francine Chisholm, who at the time worked as a Mental Health Nursing Research Advisor, conducted a needs assessment of women living with a mental illness. Many women living with a mental illness live isolated marginalized lives.

The MSS Women's Program was developed to give women the opportunity to socialize, learn about their mental illness, and coping skills, and gain positive self-esteem through activities such as participating in day-long retreats, visiting the Winnipeg Art Gallery, bowling, and going on outings to ArtBeat Studio, The Club House of Winnipeg, etcetera. Through speakers from other organizations, they have learned about women's health issues, diabetes, budgeting, and women's heart health. We've even published several booklets in the Writers' group. These booklets written by the women in the group contain stories, biographies, poetry and art. One of the authors offered these words about the experience: "I like writing, and I get a good response for it in the Writer's Group, plus I like the opportunity to have the women's writings published in the Footsteps booklets."

I recently asked the women of the Women's Group what keeps them coming back. They said: "The group provides fellowship, an opportunity to get out of the house and share our feelings and thoughts in a safe place."

"Being with other women makes me feel well."

"I feel at ease with women who understand me and don't judge me."

I also work with the Peer Support group at MSS. This group is for both men and women and gives the opportunity to learn about schizophrenia, schizoaffective disorder, anxiety disorder, obsessive-compulsive disorder, mood disorders, and manic depression. People learn how to develop coping strategies for dealing with symptoms and medication side-effects. In the Peer Support group, as well as the Women's Program, participants are given the opportunity to plan activities thereby empowering them to make choices in their lives that they may not be able to do otherwise. This can help with building confidence and self-esteem, and the comradery works well in helping people to make new friends, something that may have been lost in the process of developing schizophrenia. In the Peer Support Group, we go on outings from time to time visiting museums, The Planetarium, bowling, and the Winnipeg Hydro building. These outings help with working to eliminate the stigma of mental illness. One individual said to me. "Thank you for doing this. It's nice to be out with a group of people and not feel like people are staring at me because they think I look scary."

In both groups, we have barbeques in the summer, go on outings and get tickets to attend the Winnipeg Symphony Orchestra, etcetera.

Recovery can mean different things to different

people. For some just walking through the door for the first time takes a lot of courage. In peer support groups the comradery with other people living with a mental illness gives people opportunities to socialize, make friends and enjoy learning in a safe, non-judgmental setting.

This chapter would not be complete without giving a brief description of what schizophrenia is. Schizophrenia is a complex brain disorder whereby people have a break with reality. That does not mean that people have split personalities. There are several types of schizophrenia and a variety of symptoms. Some symptoms include delusions, hallucinations, disorganized thinking or speaking, abnormal behaviour or thinking that everyone is out to get them.

In working in the mental health field, I believe it is important to "meet people where they are at" in their journey to recovery. Being a good listener is also a key component in helping people. It doesn't take a rocket scientist to realize that if we treat people with respect and dignity, they are more likely to react in a positive manner.

I have seen a lot of personal growth in people over the years. Some people have gone on to further education or have started regular jobs again. Others have started volunteering to provide them with the opportunity to learn new skills and possibly gain future employment.

Another word about working with people living with schizophrenia, schizoaffective disorder or other mental illnesses is this. In the twenty-plus years that I've worked with people living with a mental illness, I've never encountered a person who, in a state of psychosis or a break with reality, exhibited violence in my presence. In fact, of the one per cent of the population that might be violent, 99 percent of these people are likely to be victims of violence rather than be violent against others whether this violence is by attacks from other people or by suicide. Violence is more likely to occur in a family situation.

"The statistics on sanity are that one out of every four people has a mental illness. Look at three of your friends. If they're okay, then it's you." By Rita Mae Brown.

At the Manitoba Schizophrenia Society, we believe that recovery from mental illness is possible.

We can continue to help you:

To learn to identify the symptoms of mental illness;

We can teach you and your co-workers and friends coping skills so that you will be able to teach our staff or friends how to recognize the symptoms of mental illness.

We can teach people ways to help to control those symptoms and help people learn to live normal lives and improve their working relationships.

The benefits to you and your company are:

Better working relationships

Increased productivity
Decreased sick time
And INCREASED PROFITS.

In conclusion "Hope is wishing something would happen. Faith is the belief that something will happen. Courage is making something happen."

There is always hope for recovery.

About the Author

Karen Kaplen is a Peer Support Worker with the Manitoba Schizophrenia Society. She has worked in this role for over 15 years where she facilitates support groups for people living with a mental illness.

She empowers men and women in the groups by letting them make collaborative decisions and giving them a voice. Some of her clients require help with applications for housing, obtaining food or rides to appointments, or one-on-one consultations.

In April 2016, she received the Women Helping Women award from Soroptimist International Winnipeg branch. This award is given to a woman who has made a significant contribution to improving the lives of women and children. Karen was the keynote speaker at the Soroptimist of Winnipeg Awards Presentation on April 23, 2016.

Karen is a past Area Director of Toastmasters International. She received a Distinguished Service Award for her work. A dedicated volunteer, Karen has served as President, as well as several other board positions for her club.

Karen Kaplen
kkaplen@mts.net

RULES OF ENGAGEMENT FOR ADULT CONVERSATION
BY CATHERINE KELLAR

OVERVIEW

The main motivation for writing this chapter came about as a result of years of frustrating and damaging interpersonal communication. Misunderstandings, hurt feelings and unresolved personal development issues all traced back to poor communication skills. It is hoped that this book will offer a comprehensive insight into improving your own communication and listening skills.

My personal experiences lead me to believe that boundaries must be established to enter into an ADULT CONVERSATION. These communication boundaries were created by using a rule-based framework to allow all parties fair, honest and progressive communication.

Since adopting these rules and applying them to my daily life, a marked improvement has occurred to increase the positive nature of my own interpersonal communications and relationships. These improvements have positively affected multiple areas in my life, including physical and spiritual well-being.

THESE RULES REALLY WORK!

When you initially start the process, it could be postulated that the RULES OF ENGAGEMENT FOR ADULT CONVERSATION are open to negotiation and interpretation.

THAT IS DEFINITELY NOT THE CASE!

These RULES are the cornerstone for establishing constructive verbal interaction between progressive-minded adults. Strict adherence to these RULES ensures that YOU understand and will obtain maximum benefit from working with specific communications tools.

I encourage you, as a reader to embrace these tools and use them daily, much as a carpenter would utilize a saw and hammer on the job site.

After all, you are an ADULT, aren't you?

There is no guarantee that everyone you come in contact with will be compliant and adhere to these rules. As a matter of course, the MAJORITY OF PEOPLE you interact with on a daily basis will break one or more of these rules in combinations and with regularity during the course of a conversation.

All you can do as an ADULT COMMUNICATOR is to encourage and educate others. Familiarize yourself and others by using this book to adopt and integrate this methodology in all facets of your daily life. Maximum benefit from adult conversations is obtained when these rules are APPLIED CONSISTENTLY.

The familiarization of yourself and education of other MUST originate from a place of RESPECT, LOVE, and COMPASSION. You will understand AS TIME PASSES that compassionate speaking and loving listening will allow all parties to a conversation embrace the book's methodology.

RULES OF ENGAGEMENT - FOR ADULT CONVERSATION

INTERRUPTION = ALLOW EVERYONE THEIR SAY BY REMAINING SILENT UNTIL THE SPEAKER HAS FINISHED TALKING

SELF-AWARE = STRIVE TO UNDERSTAND AND ACCEPT THAT NOTHING THAT IS SAID ABOUT YOU IS TO BE TAKEN PERSONALLY

DEFLECTION = STAY FOCUSED ON THE TOPIC BEING DISCUSSED (DO NOT ABRUPTLY CHANGE THE SUBJECT OR TONE OF THE CURRENT CONVERSATION)

MINDFULNESS = UNDERSTAND AND ACCEPT YOUR OWN EMOTIONS BY REFUSING TO DEFLECT THOSE EMOTIONS ONTO OTHERS

GOSSIP = ALLOW EACH PERSON THEIR OWN ATTITUDE BY SPEAKING ABOUT THEM ONLY IN A POSITIVE WAY

RULE #1 INTERRUPTION = ALLOW EVERYONE THEIR SAY BY REMAINING SILENT

UNTIL THE SPEAKER HAS FINISHED TALKING

This rule is important in adult conversation because it is the represented as a basic premise on which two-way intellectual conversations take place.

The application of this rule occurs in all facets of everyday life.

Examples seen in our everyday life, ranges from a structured business meeting, all the way to a casual conversation with any person communicating ideas and sharing experiences.

Two-way intellectual adult conversations are efficient and effective when the evidence of interruption or more than one voice audible at any time, DOES NOT APPEAR. A valuable lesson or "take away" should be as simple as "take your turn" when engaging with others in a conversational forum.

When adults adhere to the RULE #1 (ALLOW EVERYONE THEIR SAY BY REMAINING SILENT UNTIL THE SPEAKER HAS FINISHED TALKING), it exemplifies a courtesy - a basic form of polite behavior. Mutual respect is established immediately by including an element of trust and good will.

This framework of communication truly enhances an exchange of information and ideas for mutual benefit. The quality of life is improved with a clear understanding of concepts, beliefs and the sense of being heard by the other person.

There are negative consequences and outcomes to

a conversation when this rule is ignored or broken by one or multiple participants. Interruptions cause the conversation or message conveyed to be broken and non-cohesive. The unsolicited interruption of the Speaker quite often causes issues with an understanding of ideas or the message of the conversation initially being conveyed.

Some examples of the results or outcomes of a conversation when an interruption occurs:

The Interrupter never obtains all of the pertinent information from the Speaker's conversation. The information is lost or misinterpreted causing mistakes or a rehashing of the information at a later date.

The Speaker usually loses their train of thought, not completing the dissemination all of the information needed to explain their ideas.

The interruption caused a change in direction or flow in the Speaker's mind and can actually change the speech.

The Speaker believes the violator (Interrupter) does not respect them or their ideas.

The Speaker may have negative feelings triggered. These negative feeling can include a lack of self-worth, negative self-esteem, frustration, anger, resentment or disappointment in the Interrupting party.

The Speaker believes the Interrupter was not intently listening or considering what the Speaker had to say.

The Speaker believes the Interrupter has another agenda priority and truly does not want to consider all facets of the communication being delivered.

THE NEGATIVE STYLES OF INTERRUPTION

Not all interruptions are the same. Depending on the person interrupting, the situation of the interruption and the perception of the person being interrupted the results after the interruption can be very different. The style and delivery of an interruption can provide insight for the receiving party.

A strong and forceful interruption serves to abruptly stop the speaker from continuing with their line and direction of that specific communication. This type of interruption delivered with a loud and obnoxious fervor can be interpreted as "bullying behavior."

Simply interjecting a word or phrase you believe is "correct" if the speaker falters for a second, is an interruption. This form of "help" will change the speaker's focus and cause disruption of their speech idea.

The Interrupter actually completes the speaker's sentences for them. Unfortunately, the completed sentence may not even have anything to do with the Speaker's original idea. This type of interruption can not only disrupt the Speaker but also mislead an audience attempting to understand the Speaker's concepts.

Interruptions can also come in the form of non-verbal cues or "Body English." Rolling of the eyes, a scowl, or the subtle shaking of a head back and forth in disgust can all serve just as well to distract and disrupt the speaker.

The speaker becomes distracted or frustrated, losing their train-of-thought. These distractions also show the Interrupter is not fully immersed in the speaker's communication. Usually, their mind is focused on their own thoughts, losing the original conversation's ideas.

The interruption of another person's conversation demonstrates a number of issues with the Interrupter:

The Interrupter lacks the mature ability to remember what they wish to say after the speaker has ceased to speak. They rush in having their own say quickly and out of turn.

The Interrupter displays a childish, self-absorption with their personal thoughts. The Interrupter believes what they have to say is far more important than anyone else.

The Interrupter has a lack of interest in the speaker and their ideas or point of view. The Interrupter believes they have "heard it all before" or they have no interest in the speaker as a person or the subject being discussed.

The Interrupter "one-ups" your conversation ideas with their life experiences/ knowledge which is "bigger, better, brighter" than yours. This type of

Interrupter hijacks the conversation from the original Speaker or attempts to minimize their importance in the conversation.

The Interrupter asks questions that are going to or already have been presented by the Speaker.

THE POSITIVE OUTCOMES OF NON-INTERRUPTION

There are positive consequences and outcomes to a conversation when RULE #1 (ALLOW EVERYONE THEIR SAY BY REMAINING SILENT UNTIL THE SPEAKER HAS FINISHED TALKING) is applied or adhered to by all participants in the conversation.

These outcomes include:

Each Speaker's ideas are heard as a complete, concise concept which leads to fewer misunderstandings or the need to repeat the information.

The conversation can flow back and forth between participants freely leading to an increased creativity.

The number of questions after the speech is complete are minimal and more on target, leading to more effective and efficient information exchange.

The quality and amount of information disseminated is greatly enhanced.

Proper communication gives the Speaker an enhanced sense of self-esteem and self-worth.

The Speaker feels validated as their ideas have

been listened to completely and this leads to the development of a trusting and strong relationship between participants.

All of the above points lead to quality time management through high-level communication skills.

REMINDING YOURSELF

The most important idea to consider though out this process is the work each must do themselves. To quote Michael Jackson who sang – "I am starting with the man in the mirror," before you expect others to follow you.

To help you advance with your self-education a few reminders:

BE MINDFUL – Always keep in the front of your mind, Am I interrupting? Am I allowing this person an opportunity to speak their thoughts and ideas to the fullest? Would I cut into the front of the ticket line-up at a movie? I hope not!

KEEP IT CONCISE – There is nothing more irritating than hearing someone prattle on and on about the same thing. Makes you almost want to interrupt yourself. When it is your opportunity to speak, be aware of how long your part of the conversation is and allow others their turn. You are not giving a lecture or speech, but are part of a conversation.

KEEP SILENT – This is a very difficult practice to follow in the present day world of instant everything. If you believe you have an important, insightful comment to make, wait until the speaker has stopped talking. Acknowledge the speaker and his comment, and then state your insight in a concise, pleasant manner. Contribute to the conversation with wit, humor (if appropriate) and insight, and then allow the next speaker their say.

EMPLOY A FILTER ON YOUR COMMENTS – There are times when comments are NOT appropriate or necessary in a conversation. Learn to censor your own thoughts before you have to say "Did I say that with my outside voice?" This idea is especially important in a business setting, but even intimate exchanges can benefit from restraint.

POSSESSING SELF-CONTROL – While this may sound similar to the filtering issue, self-control is needed for all the steps in the self-aware journey. Learn to expect the best from yourself and follow the dictates of your mind to fulfill those ideas of growth.

HELPING OTHERS

Not only should you be responsible for your own education and part in the non-interruption process BUT you are responsible for teaching others the pleasure and productivity of Speech Etiquette. The more individuals that participate in the practice, the more straightforward informed discussion could occur.

EXPLAIN THE ISSUE – Gently explain to people before you speak what you expect to occur during a conversation. Outline the benefits and pleasures of good Speech Etiquette. Show them reference resources like this book. The book will help them understand what everyone should be striving to accomplish on the communication journey.

RAISE YOUR HAND, NOT YOUR VOICE – It is very important to utilize a non-aggressive body language and voice. When someone interrupts you, gently raise your hand, smile and say "Interesting comment but please allow me to finish first." Raising your voice to talk over someone increases tension and causes all participants in the conversation to be tense and freeze up. People are not receptive to ideas when they are uncomfortable.

ACTIVELY LISTEN – Really listen to the conversation, use your body to convey an interest in the speaker's ideas (smile, make eye contact, uncross your arms). Active listening allows you to hear the entire conversation, the ideas, the passion and the truth of the speaker. Your questions/ comments will be more insightful and appreciated by all the participants of the conversation.

REVIEW – When you have participated in a conversation which followed the Rule of Speech Etiquette, spend a few minutes to point out to all the participants how much was accomplished, how the emotions in the room were positive and ignited and the sheer pleasure of the moment. An awareness of the Etiquette Rules and their positive results will stimulate people to make the rules a large part of their daily communication.

This chapter only gives a short insight into the

many concepts dealing with having clear, concise and meaningful adult conversations. The different Rules of Engagement can all be delved into in a more extensive manner with workshops, keynote speeches and one-on-one counseling conducted by the author.

I welcome your interest and look forward to introducing you to more information on this subject. A true understanding and utilization of Rules of Engagement for Adult Conversations will enable you to experience a less stressful and more fulfilling lifestyle.

About the Author

Catherine is the founder and president of the consulting firm, C.K.R. KNOWLEDGE INC. She directs change and provides capacity for First Nations in Manitoba. Her advanced communication skills result in First Nations leaders implementing meaningful economic changes in their community.

She worked for over 30 years in medical research at the Universities of Manitoba and Calgary and the National Research Council. During her career, she partnered with many levels of management to coordinate and facilitate medical implementation programs that impacted people's lives.

Catherine is a member of Toastmasters International, President of the Lindenwoods Duplicate Bridge Club, Founder of the Lindenwoods Pickleball Group, and Past President of the Winnipeg Newcomers Association. She understands how to get the best out of volunteers to provide quality programs. Each of the programs she is involved with grows and thrives as a result of her leadership.

Catherine Kellar
(204) 296-5000
catherine@ckrknowledge.ca

EXECUTIVES AND IT – ON THE SAME PAGE
BY KURT PENNER

Information technology (IT) professionals often get a bad rap. TV programs and movies have portrayed them as "geeks," "nerds" or people with the inability to experience human emotions. Ask a typical executive to visualize an IT professional, and they might imagine the Big Bang Theory's Sheldon Cooper, a character that ticks each of those boxes. Not really fair – but stereotypes can create reality, especially if you don't actually know any IT people (aside from when you need to call someone to fix a printer).

The most effective and innovative organizations have this in common: there is a direct relationship between the success of the business and how well they use technology. Innovation is not just for geeks anymore. It also means having an executive team that understands technology and how it can benefit their bottom line.

I remember sitting in a meeting with the Chief Information Officer at a former company. He went over his IT Strategic Plan for the new year. There were things like upgrading the enterprise resource planning system (ERP) and centralizing our IT infrastructure resources at head office. After the meeting I was left with a question – what did any of this have to do with the direction of the overall business? We're upgrading the ERP – great! But, the missing piece was "how does this help the company?" You could easily make a case for how the new ERP would make it easier to exchange orders with customers and suppliers. The advanced production scheduler would tell our purchasing group when to order materials so they'd be ready just-in-time for manufacturing, saving millions in inventory costs. The consolidated financials would make end of year reporting over 60% quicker. These were tangible, easy to understand business benefits but unfortunately, the report focused on the what instead of the why.

Many companies have a strategic business plan which is divorced from the IT strategic plan. Successful organizations recognize they need the executive and IT to work in concert to discover opportunities to reach customers in a different way through technology.

To make these pieces fit together, both IT and business need to be able to communicate with each other. Here are five strategies you can deploy in your organizations to work together with IT, instead of around them.

1. It's not (only) about the technology.

Tech by itself is only a toy. The true challenge is figuring out how a particular technology application can help extend your market reach, better address the needs of your customers, or help improve your bottom line. IT management (especially in smaller organizations) sometimes makes the mistake of implementing "the latest cool thing" just because it's something new to learn and fun to work with. It's important for leaders to ask IT management clear questions about why they're moving forward with a particular technology, such as:

Is it easy to use/train staff on the new technology?

What impact/disruption do you anticipate to the business?

What is the start up cost? Ongoing support and maintenance costs?

Why did we decide on this particular vendor or solution?

On the flip side, for an IT manager, there is nothing worse than "I saw this demo" syndrome. I took over a position with an organization that signed a contract with a vendor to provide an application and exam tracking system. There were no business requirements in writing. And, on my first test of the software, the program ground to a screeching halt with cryptic error messages. I went to the line managers to ask why we acquired this software, and the only thing I heard was: "Oh, a few of the directors saw the demo, and they liked it." They made their decision without talking to the people who would actually have to work with the software, and the rest of us were stuck with trying to make it work. The takeaway: make sure you get both your business team and your IT group involved in the decision-making process and don't get seduced by a flashy vendor presentation.

As a leader, you may go to IT with a solution in mind, but you need to be open to look at other options that would give you what you need. Ideally, you'd like a new case management system with all the bells and whistles, but do you have the budget to get something custom developed? Maybe there's a way IT can help you leverage existing tools like MS Office or SharePoint to deliver most of what you want?

2. Speak the Same Language

One of my past supervisors had a bad habit of jumping into a situation without getting background information. I remember one meeting where we'd gathered a group of lab experts to discuss how to best share information between their lab network and a new scientific instrument. My supervisor took over the meeting right away. He talked about how they could connect the instrument to display data on a dashboard to the executives at head office, and how he could design a new piece of software to get reports. He was excited! Everyone else was confused. A few were sitting with arms crossed, resenting his "IT is coming to tell me how to run my lab" attitude. At the end of his five-minute soliloquy, he turned to one of the lab techs and said "just one question. What does this thing do?"

There's no easier way for your credibility to take a nosedive than to be exposed for not knowing what you're talking about. My supervisor found that lesson out the hard way. But, you don't have to.

As a corporate leader, your focus isn't on knowing everything about a tech solution. You don't need to know everything; you just need to be willing to ask intelligent and thoughtful questions that demonstrate you're listening and trying to understand the technology. IT professionals will respect your curiosity and interest and try to help.

If IT is presenting something to you that you're not completely processing, don't be afraid to stop and ask for clarification. Some techniques include:

- Asking IT to use diagrams and screenshots to illustrate points
- Use business analogies and examples that are simple to understand. Sometimes you need to teach IT some of your language and concepts, instead of the other way around
- Don't stay silent - if you're not sure about something, make a point of confirming your understanding with the IT group. You can use phrases like "So, based on this proposal, I understand that" to get confirmation or clarification.

3. Automation is not necessarily improvement

In more established organizations, "putting it on the computer" has been considered a magic-bullet solution that automatically makes everything faster, cheaper and more efficient. I once worked with a client who wanted customers to be able to submit application forms online. The client thought the customers would fill out their application form. Then, she would print the completed forms, and file them in the filing room. Progress!

Any process re-engineering effort needs to take into account three key things:

> 1. Are there any steps which do not add value to the end product?

Here, we are defining value as either enhancing the product or improving the quality of service to customers.

> 2. Can we eliminate waste?

Waste can sneak up on you. If you have a document that has to be approved, you may have just set off a domino effect of waste. Let's say you require a paper signature. You'd need to print the document, collate it, and walk it to someone's office. Then, the admin assistant touches the document again, reviews it, and passes it on. It sits in an inbox for a couple of weeks, until the intended recipient finally signs it. Approvals can be tricky – sure, we need to approve documents, but how many people really need to review something before you can proceed? With SharePoint, you can construct complex multi-level approval workflows. In some organizations, this can create a bunch of digital clutter where information sits stagnant in a digital "in tray."

> 3. Who does what?

Sometimes, inefficiency can be a result of not

clarifying roles and responsibilities. Maybe two or three groups are doing the same job or reviewing the same information. Is there a way we can share information and centralize processing in one key system?

A "new" process is not necessarily a "better" process. When a new supervisor started with one of my clients, the first thing he did was introduce the Excel spreadsheet for tracking he used with a previous division. He thought the new Excel sheet would make data entry more efficient for staff. Instead, it created more duplication. Data entry clerks would enter information into the new Excel sheet, but they'd still have to update the master system. Sometimes, the Excel sheet and the master system (as well as paper records) were out of date or inconsistent. A system designed to make things easier only introduced more problems.

Changing a process isn't easy. It's even harder when an "improvement" in one place creates more work for someone downstream. Everyone impacted needs to have input into the redesign. People are more likely to get excited about something they had a hand in creating, than something that's pushed on them from the outside.

Sometimes it helps to have someone from outside your main business unit (like a business analyst from IT) help your team to map out their business process and highlight where you can make improvements. An external perspective can sometimes help your team see things they've always taken for granted, and challenge "we've always done it this way before" thinking.

4. Clarify Expectations and Understand the "Triple Constraint" (Time, Scope, Resources)

You can have your project faster, cheaper, or more functional. But, you can't have all three.

On one project, I worked with a division that had recently absorbed a smaller division of the organization. The secondary division had made a public commitment they would have an online application system in three months. They made this announcement (as is usually the case) before consulting with IT to make sure this timeline was feasible.

I met with the client and outlined their options. We could do the work properly, and incorporate the online form into their other systems. This would take longer but would be a more efficient course of action. Perhaps there could be a way the messaging could be massaged to manage expectations of the external stakeholders. Another option would be to increase the budget to bring in a couple of additional programmers. Or, we could throw up a quick snap on to the other division's system. We'd create manual processes to bridge the two systems in the process and introduce inefficiencies, but you'd have it in three months. Unfortunately, the client chose to go that route. We had to cut scope significantly to meet that deadline and schedule additional work after the initial launch. We had a public-facing front end, but in the back office, there were more delays. When we did get to the integration phase, some of the work in the "quick snap in" had to be redone or redesigned. The net result was a greater cost than if we had a realistic timeline to work with.

One key mistake had happened before the project was even proposed – IT management wasn't part of the corporate decision-making process. This meant the project was "dropped" on IT without having input from IT management if it was feasible. Executives need to understand projects involve trade-offs and need to decide which of the three project drivers is most important. Sometimes getting your project done faster costs more in the long run.

5. Build Relationships

It's important to have a go-to person in IT that can cut through some of the bureaucracy and "tell it like it is." Building that relationship involves face time. It's not enough to send emails. You get your point across, but you don't really connect with the person and build trust. When you're doing all your communication by email, it's easy to not see the recipient as a human being. It can lead to more miscommunication and delay actually getting work done.

Building relationships is about connecting directly with people and having a conversation to figure out the best way you can help them meet their goals. It's also about seeing people outside of the usual work environment and connecting with them personally.

Personal relationships also remove the firewall between IT and business. You start at a point of asking "how can we help each other" rather than "how can I get around their rules." It also means that IT (through your contacts) can be consulted informally without going through a large investment of front end paperwork for something you may decide not to pursue.

If your IT contact isn't initiating quarterly reviews of projects they're working on for you, you probably should. It doesn't have to be formal or take a lot of time. You can also use your quarterly reviews to pick their brain over how to use technology to address a particular business problem. These are "anything goes" discussions where you both speak candidly about what is working, and what isn't. You can then work together with your client to map out a solution to these challenges.

Technology can help your company reach new markets, deliver services in a unique way, or communicate directly with your customers. IT strategy isn't just about IT. It's a joint effort between the entire management team (including IT) to develop IT initiatives and solutions that directly support the overall business strategy. An organization that breaks down barriers between IT and the rest of the business engages IT actively in strategic planning and builds positive trust-based relationships between IT contacts and senior executives is an organization well positioned to succeed.

About the Author

Kurt Penner, PMP has helped organizations embrace and navigate change for the past 15 years, working with teams in finance, manufacturing, and the public sector.

Although he comes from a business/IT background, much of his work has been with helping teams understand the human side of change management. Some of his successful projects include the Manitoba Provincial Nominee Program online web application, Manitoba Start's Job Matching implementation (an organization that helps new Canadians find jobs that match their skill set), and site expert supporting the Enterprise Resource Planning (ERP) system for a major Canadian pharmaceutical firm.

Kurt can deliver training workshops, leadership educational sessions, and conference keynotes/breakout sections that inform, entertain and inspire your team to action.

Kurt Penner
kurt.penner@gmail.com
204-293-8601

Laverne's Life Lessons from the Pumpkin Patch
by Laverne Wojciechowski

Peter Peter Pumpkin Eater
Had a wife and couldn't keep her
Put her in a pumpkin shell and
There he kept her very well!
--- Mother Goose nursery rhyme

Have you ever thought how big that pumpkin would be? Second thing maybe you thought is why did Peter Pumpkin Eater put his wife in a pumpkin shell? It's probably not a good idea in this day and age. Well, I grow pumpkins that big. Yes. Yes, I do. The most recent pumpkin I grew weighed in at 564 lbs.

I have been growing pumpkins for many years and competitively for almost 20 years. I realized during this time how things I learned in pumpkin patch apply to all areas of life. Sure some people think it is just simple gardening. To grow giant vegetables requires your attention and lots of care which needs to be giant as well. You can't just put a seed in the ground and expect the resulting fruit to be big.

So what did I learn that applies to all areas of life? How to care for something. What hard work means. Doing your best. How to compete. Making it work. Don't quit. It is about the journey, not the destination.

Lesson 1: Caring for something

Having a garden is a great way to learn how to care for something. You need to learn what the plants need in terms of water, sunlight, growing medium, and nutrients. You learn what needs to be done for the plants. Every day there is something to do whether it is watering or weeding, especially for giant pumpkins. Remembering to cover them in spring when there is a risk of frost. Pollinating the flowers to ensure the fruit sets. Keeping records of the pollinations done. Sheltering the pumpkin when it's as tall as the leaves. Dealing with any pests. Positioning the fruit, so it doesn't grow over the vine and cut off its supply of nutrients. There is constant care involved during the growing season.

People are like gardens. You need to figure what they need as well when you are caring for them, whether they are babies, teenagers, or seniors. Each type of person is at a different stage in life, and each may have different needs. You need to figure out what their needs are when you are caring for them and tend to them accordingly.

Lesson 2: Work Hard

Being lazy is easy. Many people take the easy way out. This is the road to going nowhere. If you are doing what you love and are passionate about it, you will put in the hard work – oh and by the way it won't feel like work – it will feel like play. It may look like work to others, but to you, it won't feel that way. That's the difference between doing something you love and something you don't love. You will put in the work, and it won't feel like work, it will feel like play, and you will spend hours at it.

Working hard also means showing up or doing something when you don't want to. It is amazing how good you feel once you start – because it is something you love doing. Yes, it's difficult, but not everything is easy. This also applies to promises. If you promised something for someone, then follow through. Don't promise and never show up.

I had no means of getting water to the pumpkin this year other than carrying it by hand. I didn't let that stop me. It was hard work – water is heavy! I love growing my pumpkins, so I didn't let that stop me. I put in the hard work, and I had a little help from mother nature with a few rain showers. Guess what? I grew a pumpkin that beat my personal best!

Lesson 3: Do your best

Do your best - that's only thing you can go home with for sure at the end of the day. When you think about it, that is all you can do. If you are competing, it is the one thing you can control. You can't control the judges, weather, or other competitors. You can only control you, so why not be the best you can be. There can only be one winner in a contest (unless there is a tie) and there are many "losers." Or a more positive way to think of it, many did their best that day but didn't get an award for it – and that's what they can go home with, the knowledge and satisfaction they did their best.

There is more to it though. You need to do your best all the time, no matter what. Put your heart into it. You don't know who is watching or what effect you have on others. Some people think they are lucky, but sometimes it is because they were doing their best all along and an opportunity came that took advantage of the fact they were doing their best. As for affecting others, sometimes you do not even know you are a role model or are setting an example, and others are watching. Wouldn't you want to be doing your best when they are watching?

Little did the grower of the 972lb pumpkin know that he inspired our family to grow bigger pumpkins when we saw him at our first weigh-off back in 1998. You never know who is watching and who you are inspiring.

Lesson 4: How to compete

Why compete? If you are competing to win, great, but there is so much more to competition than just winning. I compete with giant pumpkins (and in my other hobbies) to beat my personal best, i.e. get better, and to meet other people interested in my hobbies. I know there will be much, much bigger pumpkins out there. If I can do better than the previous personal best, I am happy. Competing makes you set goals. When you set goals, you challenge yourself to get better.

How do you compete? First, find the rules for the competition. Study the rules. Learn the rules. Learn the skills you will need. The rule book will tell you what is and is not allowed or acceptable and this will help you determine the limits and push the limits. Go in with the mindset to do your best. Treat your competitors with respect. Congratulate them on doing their best. Remember to learn from the experience and take away all the positives even if you don't win the hardware.

I always make a point of congratulating not only the winner but the other competitors as well. Even if I just give them a compliment. They worked hard too and deserved respect as well.

Lesson 5: Make it work

You need to do the work. Things will go wrong, not go the way you want, or go completely off track. You have to guide and put things back in the direction you want them to go. It means doing the things you need to do. It means showing up when you don't feel like it. This goes for exercising, doing the dishes, writing a speech – just do it. Once you start, you will get into it and be happy you started.

What if you run into problems? Well, you need to figure out the solution. There are many places where the whole pumpkin growing thing can go wrong. Seeds don't germinate. Tractor won't start. You get frost one night. Hail damages the plants. You anticipate the problems as best you can and deal with it – you make it work. Many people ask how are you going to lift the pumpkin if it is bigger than 1000 lbs?

I know I will deal with it if that ever happens. I will be monitoring the weight and figure it out well before it needs to be lifted out of the garden.

The great thing about making it work is you learn so much. It forces you to research and learn. It forces you to deal with the problems. Who knew I would learn how to haul a trailer, hook up a trailer, and learn how to lift heavy objects in addition to growing pumpkins?

Lesson 6: Don't quit

It is easy to throw in the towel and just give up when things are not going your way. Really easy. It's the easy way out. There are many factors that contribute to quitting including age, gender, friends, and circumstances.

Don't let age stop you! Do not let anyone tell you that you are too young or old to do anything! Pumpkin growers range in age from kids to seniors. Some "kids" are still helping their "senior" parents grow the big one in this hobby. If you have the will and capability to do something, then do it! I resumed ice skating at the age of 25, taking lessons with the little kids. Once I got the basic skills back, I progressed to the more advanced levels. It was a short awkward time to be in the beginner class but it passed, and I soon was where I wanted to be. Then I was competing in recreational adult skating in my mid-thirties – a time when most competitive skaters were packing it in and becoming professional skaters. I was enjoying the travel and meeting other people that loved to ice skate!

Don't let gender stop you! Pumpkin growing tends to have more male than female participants. It doesn't matter if you are female or male! I remember overhearing a conversation between two pumpkin growers, a female, and a male. I remember the comment by the male "But you're just a girl!" Really! This "girl" grew pumpkins over 1800lbs! Do what you love to do!

I think I got that mindset from my dad, who at 82 was still working on building a log house as his retirement project. He thought as long as he was able to do the work, why can't he keep going with his dream? What else was he going to do? Sit in front of the TV and wither away? He kept busy all the time, working on some project. He didn't quit. He didn't give up.

Don't let friends stop you! Sometimes people hold you back. You want to hang out with your friends, but sometimes they are not interested in your hobbies. Some may even be jealous to see you exceed. Some may feel embarrassed for you or that it is inappropriate for someone your age, but you don't feel that way. Sometimes loser friends will drag you down with them. When I was coaching, I don't know how many times I saw that kids would not participate if their friends were not there. They were great at the sport and might have excelled in it, but they quit because their friends were not in it anymore. None of my close friends grow giant pumpkins for competition, and that's okay. They love that I do and support me – that's the way it should be.

Don't let circumstances stop you! Things may not be going your way today but that doesn't mean tomorrow, next week, or even next year it will be the same. There may be a delay. Like the construction sign in summer says "expect delays." My tractor always acts up in the spring just when it's time to till the pumpkin patch. It always takes a while to get it fixed. Always does. I plan well ahead so if there is a delay I will get the seeds in on time. Even while building a new house I decided to still grow the giant pumpkin. This meant travelling every day to the pumpkin patch and hauling water. I don't let my circumstances rule me. I rule them.

Lesson 7: It's about the journey, not the destination.

Ever notice how excited you are when planning a vacation (i.e. destination). Then when the vacation is done, the excitement is over. The excitement happens while you are planning, travelling and enjoying (i.e. the journey). It's about the journey and not so much the destination.

The same is true for me when I grow the pumpkin and finally take it to the weigh-off. The weigh-off is just the end point of the growing season (the destination). Everything leading up to the weigh-off is the journey. The challenges in germination, planting, weeding, watering, weather, and transportation are all part of the journey. I learn throughout the growing season. Seeing the pumpkins grow through the eyes of others was an eye-opener for me this year. They were so happy and curious to see such giant pumpkins. I would give them seeds to try it for themselves.

Speaking of journeys, who knew growing giant pumpkins would allow me to travel the world? On February 24, 2016, I left for the Great Pumpkin Commonwealth conference and awards dinner called "The Big Show" in Lymington, England. Over 90 enthusiastic pumpkin growers from 13 countries descended upon Lymington to hear the basics of growing giant pumpkins, watering methods, growing other giant vegetables, and meet some of the top growers in the world. Never, never, never, did I think that doing something that I love, like growing giant pumpkins, would have me travel. Never did it cross my mind.

Summary

I grow giant pumpkins! Oh yeah, I know you are smiling when you read this sentence. People always do when I say it in person. I love it when you share your hobby, and you can bring joy to others.

Here's the thing. Pumpkin growing is a hobby for me. I like gardening. Why not grow a big vegetable to challenge myself? I keep growing pumpkins. I go to the weigh-offs. I was nominated for Great Pumpkin Commonwealth board. The board decided to hold a conference in England. I went to England .... because I grow giant pumpkins!!!!

So why am I sharing all this? What started out as something I did to help my dad, turned into a hobby. I learned many life lessons from spending time in the pumpkin patch. I ultimately travelled to England, the first place I wanted to goes overseas.

Who knew growing giant pumpkins would get me to a place I always wanted to go. I even appeared on a local radio show to talk about my trip to England and the pumpkins! You never know what life has in store and how one thing will lead to another or who you will meet along the way. That is why you always need to do your best and put your heart into everything you do. You never know who is watching and what influence they will have on your journey, or what influence you will have on other people. And you know what? It's all about the journey and not so much the destination. Did I ever grow the biggest pumpkin, NO? Did I ever win a weigh-off, NO? But I still keep growing pumpkins! It's all about the fun and the journey.

Guess what? All these lessons above can be applied to have a successful life. Whatever you define as success is up to you, because it is different for everyone, but the common things between successful people are the seven lessons above.

I keep growing giant pumpkins because I love to garden and I want to beat my personal best, that is being successful for me. It is not about winning the contest but about participating and doing your best. I love when people come to my yard, see the giant pumpkins and they can't believe it! I love when, everywhere I go, I mention I grow giant pumpkins, and they smile!

If you are having a down day, remember it can

get worse. Look at a pumpkin and smile!

For more information on giant pumpkins visit bigpumpkins.com and greatpumpkincommonwealth.com.

About the Author

Laverne is a dynamic, entertaining speaker who will have your audience laughing and inspired to accomplish their goals. Laverne believes in leading by example, becoming the role model for the organization.

Laverne has over 25 years of experience in the scientific field, but gardening is one of her favourite hobbies. She has been growing giant pumpkins (some over 500 lbs!) most of her life. She shares her experiences in the pumpkin patch and how those experiences, applied to your personal life and business, will make your personal life bloom and will make your business flourish and grow. She believes in cultivating the power of positive thinking for personal growth.

Laverne believes communication skills are important in everyday life and it's not just what you say but the visual clues that are important as well.

Laverne Wojciechowski
wojciech@mymts.net

DISCOVER THE MAGIC OF BELIEVING IN YOU
BY GREG WOOD

I remember being sixteen years old and the time had come for me to decide what I wanted to do for a living. I decided that I wanted to be a Professional Land Surveyor. The reason I had to decide so young was that I would have to go to college for that profession and I had to set myself up for the right courses for my senior year so that I could get into college. It is hard to believe that I had to set my career goal at 16 even if I wouldn't get there until I was 26. I met that goal and became a partner in the premiere Land Surveying firm in Manitoba by the time I was 30.

I met that goal. But let me ask you a question. Why is it that some people reach their goals and others do not? What determines a person's success? What determines whether they will reach their goals or not?

If we were to ask these questions of those who had achieved their goals we might get answers like these:

Stay in school. Get a good education. Go to

University.

Find a job you like and stick with it. Keep your nose to the grindstone. Work hard, and you'll get ahead.

Building the right relationships is important. After all, you know what they say, "It's not what you know, it's who you know."

Getting an education, working hard, and building relations are all important, but they are small in comparison to one's self-image. The greatest separator between successful and unsuccessful people throughout any stage of life is how they perceive themselves.

You see, we don't get out of life what we want. That's called a dream. The reason people feel that dreams don't come true is that what they get out of life is directly proportional to how they see themselves.

We can't reach our dream with a low self-esteem.

Allow me to explain it this way. Think of your self-esteem as a ten dollar bill. How much is it worth? Ten dollars. That's right we can use it to buy ten dollars worth of stuff. The point is everyone knows the value of it.

But suppose we reach into our wallet one day and find that it has changed into a five dollar bill. Its worth to the world would be only five dollars. We could only purchase five dollars worth of goods with it. We have given it a low value, and the world is

NOT going to increase that value for us. We may have ten dollar plans for it, but it doesn't matter because we can't get more than five dollars for it.

Our self-esteem is the value we put on ourselves. If we have a goal that is a 10 but the value we have placed on ourself is a 5, we'll never achieve that 10 goals. Just like the five dollar bill in the example above, if we give it a low value, the world is not going to increase it for us.

We can't buy $10 worth of groceries with a $5 bill;

We can't win a 10K race if we can only run 5K; and

We can't reach a 10 dream with a five self-image

Nathaniel Branden, a psychotherapist, and author of the book Six Pillars of Self-Esteem say:

"Of all the judgments you make in life, none is as important as the one you make about yourself. The difference between low self-esteem and high self-esteem is the difference between passivity and action, between failure and success."

"The level of our self-esteem has profound consequences for every aspect of our existence: how we operate in the workplace, how we deal with people, how high we are likely to rise, how much we are likely to achieve--and in the personal realm, with whom we are likely to fall in love, how we interact with our spouse, children, and friends, what level of personal happiness we attain."

There is almost no area of our life that is not impacted by how we perceive ourselves.

In fact, people who believe in themselves get better jobs than those with low self-esteem. They also perform better in those jobs.

Martin Seligman, psychology professor at the University of Pennsylvania, did some research at the Metropolitan Life insurance company and found that the salespeople who were optimists outsold the pessimists by 31 percent.

The impact of belief in self-begins early. Some researchers assert that when it comes to academic achievement in school, there is a greater correlation between self-confidence and achievement than there is between IQ and achievement.

The good news is, we CAN increase our self-esteem. We do not have to be stuck at a 5. We can raise our self-image from a five to a ten.

And we can shoot for that ten dream.

I want to be clear that this is not an "If you can believe it, you can achieve it" message because that's just not true. But we will never be able to climb the ladder to success if our self-esteem keeps us on the bottom rung.

"You can succeed in life if nobody else believes in you, but you will never succeed if you don't believe in yourself." William J. H. Boetcker

I am going to share five steps to raise your own

self-esteem. Together they form a M.A.G.I.C formula for growing self-esteem.

I was a professional land surveyor for over 20 years, and I saw a lot of strange things working in that field. I remember being in a farm yard, one day, watching as a cow bent low to the ground, turned her head sideways, pushed it forward, and started to eat some grass. I asked the farmer if the cow had received a recent blow to her head. He laughed and said, "No, there just used to be a fence there." She had become so conditioned to the fence being there that she didn't even notice that it was gone.

Have you ever seen an invisible fence? I guess that's a pretty stupid question because if you've seen it, then it's not invisible. I remember setting up for a friend's wedding in someone's backyard. They overlooked a golf course and had a large area behind them to host a wedding. However, the neighbours had a dog and no fence. As I saw him come bounding over, I could see we would have trouble keeping the food safe. But he stopped. For no reason, he just stopped and didn't come any closer. His owner told me that it was because they had installed an invisible fence. They had buried a wire underground, and the dog wore a collar that would buzz when he got close to it. If he moved forward, he would get a mild shock, reminding him to stay in his own yard. As he approached the fence, the shock would get more severe. His fear of that shock kept him in his yard.

I have been in the same position myself. I have

moved toward a goal, but as I got near the edge of my comfort zone, I stopped. My self-limiting beliefs kept me where I was. I did not believe in myself enough. My fear of failure was stronger than my desire to succeed.

It goes quite far back in my life. I studied theatre for several years as a teenager, but I could never pull the trigger and give it a real shot because it was easier and safer to just go to college and work a regular job for regular pay.

At the age of 20, I was going to be a standup comic and open for a pair of Elvis impersonators and tour the east coast of the US. I had about two hours of routines ready, but as I hit the edge of my comfort zone, I stopped. It turned out to be another dream that I didn't follow through on. It just seemed like such a risk. And failure was a real possibility. What if I wasn't funny enough? What if I bombed? I had just graduated college, and I had a good job. How could I risk that?

Have you ever done that? Got to the edge of your comfort zone and stopped? That is a self-limiting belief.

As leadership guru John Maxwell says, "The greatest limitations people experience in their lives are usually the ones they impose upon themselves."

It is important to remember not to believe everything you think. You must ask yourself why you think that. Why do you believe that about yourself? Is it true? What could I do if that wasn't true?

By the way, we bought an invisible fence, and I installed it around our yard, but it didn't work on our dog. His desire to leave the yard was stronger than his fear of the pain. He would just grit his teeth and pushed through.

I remember thinking, as I am watching him run toward the edge of the yard, get that jolt and keep going! "What a stupid dog." But as I look back on it, I really wish I had learned that valuable lesson from him. It really is worth it to move beyond my self-limiting beliefs.

So step number one and the M in MAGIC is to:

Move past your limiting beliefs.

Many people with a low self-image become selfish and self-centered. They start to focus on themselves and their problems which only increases the problem.

The best way to turn those feelings around is to reach out and help someone else. Spend time volunteering with the less fortunate. It is hard to feel bad about yourself when you are doing good for someone else.

Adding value to someone else, even in a small way, will lift your self-esteem.

Our daughter, who usually has a very positive self-image, had some things go wrong in her life at the same time, and it started to affect her self-esteem. She had lost her job, and she was questioning her own value. It was holding her back.

So she started to volunteer at a local soup kitchen, and the turn around in her was almost immediate. She felt much better about herself, and she was the recipient of so much gratitude from the people she was helping and the people with whom she served. They valued her service, and that caused a cycle of positive feelings from them to her. Also, her positive feelings spill over to her clients who feel better just talking with her.

In the early 50's Don Clifton was teaching psychology at the University of Nebraska when he noticed a problem. The entire field of psychology was based on studying what was wrong with people. So he decided to explore what is right with people. He and his team interviewed over a million people and found that every interaction we have with another individual either adds to us or subtracts from us. He was the first to use the terms the bucket and the dipper.

Clifton claims that everyone has an invisible bucket and when it is full we feel good about ourselves. When it is empty, we feel bad.

Every human interaction we have, whether it is ordering a cup of coffee or spending time with a loved one, either adds to or subtracts from that bucket.

Each one of us also has an invisible dipper, and that dipper can be used to dip into someone else's bucket or used to fill someone else's bucket.

The interesting thing that Dr. Clifton found was when you use your dipper to dip into someone else's bucket, you dip into your own as well. But when you use your dipper to fill someone else's bucket, you are actually filling your own bucket as well.

And this is not something new. Over 3000 years ago, King Solomon of Israel, thought by many to be the wisest man who ever lived, said. "When you are kind to others, you are kind to yourself, when you are cruel to others, you are cruel to yourself."

Do you remember the ice bucket challenge of a few years ago? It raised a lot of money for charity.

I have a new bucket challenge for you today. This one won't raise any money, but it can sure raise your self-esteem. My challenge to you is to spend time filling your bucket by filling the buckets of others.

The second step and the A in MAGIC is:

Add value to others.

Sticks and stones will break my bones, but names will never hurt me. What a load of bull.

Everybody has found themselves the victim of name calling at least once in their lives. Sometimes this is done out of jest, and sometimes it is done in a deliberate move to be mean to another person.

This kind of name calling can be very hurtful, but it pales in comparison to the things we say to ourselves.

Even though many of us are not aware of it, we are talking to ourselves all the time. And the things we tell ourselves are either positive or negative. We either build ourselves up, or we tear ourselves down. How about you? Are you creating a positive self-image? Or are you saying things that diminish your self-image?

Do you think or worse say things like, "I'm no good at remembering names?"

I used to say that all the time. And because I said it, I believed it. I would meet someone new and wouldn't even really try to remember their name. I didn't work at it at all. When I saw somebody I had met before, I didn't remember their name. This just confirmed in my mind that I was not good at names and the cycle repeated itself. It became a self-fulfilling prophecy.

Do you say to yourself things like:

- Am I not good enough?
- I don't belong?
- Am I not smart enough?
- No one likes me?

There is a saying, "As a man thinks in his heart, so is he." You are what you think. So I stopped saying, "I'm not good with names, and I started to say, "I'm getting better at remembering names." I worked at it. When I did remember a name, I felt good about it. I congratulated myself.

Stop saying negative things to yourself. Instead say, "I am good enough, smart enough and I belong here."

The number one thing we can do to raise our self-esteem and the G in MAGIC is to:

Guard your self-talk.

Having the integrity to do the right thing is a great way to build self-esteem. When we have done what we know is right, we get a feeling of satisfaction. This helps us feel good about ourselves.

The opposite is true when we do what we know to be wrong. When we fail to do the right thing we feel guilty. And when we experience guilt we have a diminished sense of self-worth. Also, when we regret what we have done we tend not to evaluate our mistakes, and then we don't learn from them.

Practicing even a little discipline can help to grow one's self-esteem.

A few months ago, I decided to start getting up a half hour earlier every day to make more time for reading and personal growth. I am not a 'morning person, ' so this was not an easy task. However, I knew that I needed to do this to grow. So just by forcing myself at first (and with the help of my wife) I actually started to enjoy it. Not only was I investing more time in personal growth but I also felt good that I was sticking to this new habit. I had a double win.

"Being true to yourself and your values is a tremendous self-esteem builder. Every time you take action that builds your character, you become stronger as a person—the harder the task, the greater the character builder." John Maxwell

While it is not possible to feel ourselves into

action, we can act ourselves into feeling better.

William James, the father of modern psychology, said, "We do not sing because we are happy; we are happy because we sing."

The fourth step and the I in MAGIC is:

Insist on integrity

Let me ask a question.

Do you believe you are special? I mean special, unique, extraordinary.

Let's consider three different people and compare how special they are.

First, we have Mr. Superstar. The guy who doesn't even have to try. If he were a basketball player, he would be Michael Jordan. If he were a hockey player, he would be Sidney Crosby. He is the kind of guy who makes everyone else feel insignificant.

Then we have Mr. So-So. He is not the biggest; he's not the smallest. He's not the fastest. He's not the slowest. He's not the smartest; he's not the dumbest. He's just your run of the mill, ordinary, everyday average guy. It doesn't sound like much, but I'd rather be average than a few sandwiches short of a picnic if you know what I mean.

And lastly, we have Mr. Small Fry. Talk about a few sandwiches short of a picnic; this guy couldn't even find the picnic. He's the kind of guy, who, at lunchtime, ties his French fries in knots and puts ketchup on his shoelaces.

I don't know which one of these you relate to, but there is a problem. It is not whether we are Mr. or Mrs. Small Fry, or Mr. So-so, or even Mrs. Superstar. The problem is that we compare ourselves to other people.

Comparing yourself to others has no benefit. Whether we think we are superior or inferior to them is irrelevant. The only one you should compare yourself to is you. Have you grown at all since last year, last month, other even last weekend?

The fifth step and the C in MAGIC is:

Compare you to you.

To increase your own self-esteem:

M - Move past your limiting beliefs
A - Add value to others
G - Guard your self-talk
I - Invest in integrity
C - Compare you to you

That is the M.A.G.I.C. formula for believing in you.

Remember, real Magic is believing in yourself. If you can do that, you can accomplish almost anything

About the Author

Greg Wood, the EnterTrainer, works with organizations that want to Levitate their effectiveness, make problems Vanish, and watch profits Appear.

Greg is an award winning magician, comedian, and speaker who has presented in ten countries, on five continents.

After 20 years of running a professional land surveying business Greg felt called to add value to others in another way - to help them raise their leadership, increase productivity and profitability. He changed career and worked with Leader Impact Group as a trainer and event producer, and became a Certified Speaker, Coach, and Teacher with the John Maxwell Team.

Greg's ability to blend these experiences with his unique talents as a comedy entertainer makes him a refreshing, substantive, and valuable resource for those seeking to increase their influence

Greg Wood
204-779-8066
Greg@GregWood.ca

FINDING YOUR PASSION THROUGH SERVICE
BY DAVID WOODCOCK

What are you passionate about? Is it your family? Is it your friends and those close to you? Your job? The things you own? Your community? Where do your priorities lay today?

In our busy lives, we often lose sight of what gives us the greatest joy.

In this chapter, I will inspire you to "make a difference" in the lives of those close to you, and to those whom you have never met. I want to share with you how I found my passion through serving my community.

I grew up in a normal family of six, one brother and two sisters, in southern Ontario. We were taught as young children to respect our parents and listen to their direction (aka strict). We were not "perfect" children; however, we took our schooling and relationships with each other, our friends and peers, seriously. We were well-grounded; we were expected to do our chores around the house, go to school every day, go to church on Sundays, sing in the choir, and attend Sunday school. I continued my life journey finishing Grade 13, and then on to college. In Ontario, to prepare for university, I had to attend Grade 13 unless I was going to pursue a "trade." Grade 13 had all the advanced sciences; chemistry, biology, physics, and advanced math.

After graduating, I moved to Manitoba at the age of 21. I answered an advertisement in the National Globe and Mail paper for a position with Atomic Energy of Canada Limited, a Federal Government Crown corporation located in Pinawa, Manitoba. I lived in Pinawa until 1985. Pinawa was a great town to live for families, except I was single in a government-run town. The prospect of meeting someone single for a relationship was slim to none.

I moved to Winnipeg in 1985 and lived there until I found property in Lockport, Manitoba in 1989. Lockport is situated about 20 minutes northeast of Winnipeg.

While living in Lockport, enjoying my 8.14 acres of property, I had heard the Winnipeg Folk Festival was looking for volunteers. Each year the festival is held at Bird's Hill Park, about 10 minutes from my home. The Festival promotes less-known musical artists from around the world to play various venues in the park. I had not attended the Festival until I decided to volunteer.

I was looking to expand my knowledge and become more involved in my surroundings in the community. I sent my application to the Festival Office, and a few weeks later I heard from the Volunteer Coordinator. I was placed on my second choice for crews: Festival Campground Security. On my application, I stated I had two years of security experience at my college pub (Frosty's).

During the 1996 festival, I was a model volunteer. I showed up for my shifts; I did extra shifts, and I performed very well in my duties. The following year I was asked to be a supervisor. Back then, the Supervisor was called "Big Toe." I would coordinate a small team of up to 20 volunteers to patrol the Festival Campground at various 4 to 8-hour shifts around the clock. There were several incidents that year, and I was observed as handling them correctly without further incident. My time commitment was about 80 hours that year. In 1998 I became a Coordinator for the crew. This was a big step at the time. However, I knew I could contribute more, and it was fun! I relished in the opportunity to be a leader on the team.

For several years, I barely saw or heard the music happening on the Festival Site side. The Festival Campground was situated across the road and a kilometer from the site. My passion for helping the festival grew immensely. I didn't care that I didn't hear the music because I knew I had a more important role than satisfying my own needs, like listening to the music. After all, the drumming sessions in the campground were enough musical entertainment to keep me enthused.

The crew grew from 100 to 220 volunteers from the time I started volunteering until my last year. The demands on the team became greater and greater. The Festival Office decided to start a full day earlier (Wednesday) which increased my commitment in the field. Peaceful solutions to problems in the Festival Campground were utmost important and was our goal for everything we did as a team. As the team leader, there were difficult times in disciplining some volunteers and in some cases pulling their passes (credentials), so they could not participate in the Festival.

Volunteering meant the world to me. I also knew it meant the world to the organization. My contribution exceeded 800 hours of volunteer time in an 8-9 month timeframe. I felt preparation for each four-day festival was crucial for success. At the time I said "yes," I didn't realize the time commitment I had made to serve. My passion carried me all the way to 2008. It also helped develop some wonderful long time relationships and personal growth among other volunteers.

One day just after the Festival had ended for another year; a colleague asked me: "why do you volunteer so much"? "What do you get out of it?" I vividly remember telling him it brings me great joy to help other people, and an organization I believed in. I knew he couldn't totally comprehend what I was saying to him because he hadn't volunteered much of anything in his life. I also said there are some wonderful benefits of volunteer service. For example,

- Helping individuals and the organization reach goals.
- Helping yourself (how do you feel after you

contribute?)
- Joy in knowing I made a difference.
- Meeting new people (networking).
- Learning a new skill, or skills.
- Learning to work toward a common goal/ objective/ outcome.
- Feeling part of a team.
- Relieving stress in your life.
- Being recognized as doing a great job (reward).

The experience also taught me not everyone has the same passion for helping. Volunteers are not created equal. The goal(s) may be very clear; however, some may think differently on how to achieve that goal(s). If you work to your high standard, with passion, integrity, honesty, respect, leading by example, others can see you as a model for themselves to do more, or work better in the team. I feel we all have a passion for something; it is knowing what it is and acting on it in a positive and productive way.

Finally, after 13 Festivals, it was time. I had built a strong leadership team to carry on the mission. I knew I had done all I could do to make the team better, working cohesively on a shift by shift (frontlines) basis. In 2008, I left the Winnipeg Folk Festival.

My plate had become very full. In 2004, during the time volunteering I was also going to the University of Manitoba; had a full-time job; was part of a team of setting premiums for employee health benefits; I was married with three stepchildren, and had over 8 acres of land.

However, during my time of volunteer service I came to know, those with the most on their plate, seem to find the time to get things done.

Do you agree? If you want something done, give it to the busiest person you know.

"Finding your passion through service."

In 2010, after living in Lockport for 21 years, an opportunity came to me from a good friend in Lockport to help plan for a 100th Anniversary Celebration of the St. Andrews Lock and Dam. This structure is only one of two in the world; France has a very similar constructed dam. The dam is own by the Federal Government. The celebration was being planned as an initiative of the Lockport Community Marketing Corporation (LCMC) – a Not-For-Profit Organization.

I attended my first meeting of the celebration committee. The committee consisted of local business owners, residents, and local officials from the two municipal governments. The meeting was well run, and there was input from everyone in attendance. They made me feel I belonged. I came away from the meeting thinking there was something missing. The next meeting I spoke a little more, and I came to know others around the table. Then it hit me, the celebration committee, and the LCMC were almost one and the same. The same volunteers planning the celebration were also on the Board of the LCMC. In itself, this was not a bad arrangement; however, I felt there needed to be a more visible division. The Celebration Committee needed to work more independently from the LCMC. I would address this later with more clarification.

It was clear the LCMC needed a Mission, Vision, and Values to help determine if this was something within the direction the corporation wanted to go. Meaning, they had to understand "where the corporation had been, where it was today, and where it was going in the future." A Mission statement is a statement that gives the organization direction or purpose. A Vision is what has to happen for the mission statement to hold true. Values help to guide the leaders into action; what is important.

After the second meeting, I went away and prepared what I thought would be a good Mission, Vision, and Values for the corporation. I circulated my "notes" to a couple of close friends who sat on the Board. They believed I was "onto something." I shared my thoughts on direction for the corporation and the committee at the next meeting. Everyone weighed-in on what I had prepared; it was met with a lot of discussion. We came to a consensus on the direction of the anniversary celebration, and more work to do on the bigger picture of the corporation.

I started to feel like I was appreciated for my ideas. I was valued for my contributions. I was making a difference. The people sitting around the table had very successful businesses in Lockport and the surrounding areas. I continued to attend several meetings leading up to the celebration. I remember going to each municipality and asking for funding for our anniversary celebration. With a clear vision, I was able to secure $10,000 from each municipality.

The festival celebration in 2010 was magnificent! We had three sites for top level entertainers with elaborate stages, a heritage center display area, food vendors, children's crafts, face-painting and more. The Saturday night was capped off with a fireworks show that could rival Canada Day Celebrations! Our festival and the organization were the talk of Lockport. The biggest drawback was we were not successful financially. After all the bills were paid we lost $50,000. It was good the LCMC Board members, who owned businesses, could offset the cost with short-term loans.

The experience in organizing such a big event and helping to lead it was a huge accomplishment. I learned in the following years to scale back the festival to one site and hire lesser-known musical acts to save money. I also learned to have more activities available for a minimal cost. By year four, we started to "break-even" on income/ expenses.

By 2012, I had been asked to consider the Chairman of the Board of Directors for the corporation. Given everything going on in my life I had to carefully consider what this could me for me, and the corporation. It was clear the influential majority saw something in me. They wanted my time, my speaking abilities, my organizational skills, and my leadership. It seemed like the right "fit";

however was I ready?

Have you ever considered yourself as a leader? Someone who could persuade others to follow you? I believe we all have this ability in each of us. We all have experiences where we can help each other. When the opportunity arises when the door is opened ever so slightly, do you walk through, or do you close the door?

I knew if I took this challenge, it would teach me so much about business, and more about me. It would also strengthen the relationships I had already started with community leaders, municipal governments and beyond. The door was opened, and I ran through the opening.

To this day, I continue to grow in a meaningful way in my community.

"Finding your passion through service" is all about you taking the time to find yourself and applying yourself to the betterment of a goal. Don't worry that you may not be "perfect" or "what do I have to offer." It all starts with one word "YES." In the end, you may not find yourself the Chairperson of a corporation, or the leader of a team 200 strong, but what you will find is you have enriched your life and the lives of those you have come in contact with through service.

Immerse yourself in service toward a goal or cause. I know you will be glad you did.

I want to leave you with two inspiring quotations, one from Mahatma Gandhi and the other from Sir

Winston Churchill:

"The best way to find yourself is to lose yourself in the service of others."

"We make a living by what we get; we make a life by what we give."

I will help you to FIND YOUR PASSION THROUGH SERVICE!

About the Author

David is a professional nuclear materials specialist with Canadian Nuclear Laboratories, formerly Atomic Energy of Canada Ltd, in Pinawa, Manitoba.

In his 35-year career, he worked in both nuclear and scientific operations. David has published over 25 technical papers on the underground geology of the Lac du Bonnet Batholith.

David is an inspirational and motivational leader. He served the Winnipeg Folk Festival for 13 years as Campground Security Coordinator and Safety Coordinator for 220 volunteers.

In 2010, he joined the Lockport Community Marketing Cooperation, serving as executive director and Chairman of the Board. He was a founder of the annual "Lockport Dam Family Festival."

David has two Distinguished Toastmaster designations and has delivered more than 500 speeches. He has held several District 64 leadership positions and is currently working toward his Accredited Speaker Designation.

"Finding Your Passion Through Service" is his inspiration to the world.

David R. Woodcock
Email: Woodys@mymts.net

Contact Information

http://keystonespeakers.ca/

Michael Bayer
Phone: (204) 237-9257
Toll-Free: 1-888-551-5592
Email: michael@theleanconsultinggroup.com
www.theleanconsultinggroup.com

Emma Frost
info@ruleyourworld.ca
www.ruleyourworld.ca
www.emma-frost.com
facebook | LinkedIn | Twitter /canleadtraining

Man Doan
Exploring Your Potential
Winnipeg, MB, CANADA
man@mandoan.com
www.ManDoan.com

Karen Kaplen
kaplen@mymts.net

Catherine Kellar
C.K.R. Knowledge Inc.
Winnipeg, MB, CANADA
(204) 296-5000
catherine@ckrknowledge.ca
www.ckrknowledge.ca

Kurt Penner
kurt.penner@gmail.com
(204) 293-8601

Laverne Wojciechowski
Email: wojciech@mymts.net

Greg Wood
TheMagicOfLeadership.com
Winnipeg, MB, CANADA
(204) 779-8066
Email: Greg@GregWood.ca
www.GregWood.ca
LinkedIn: theentertrainer
Facebook: EnterTrainerGregWood
Twitter: @GregWoodCanada

David R. Woodcock
Email: Woodys@mymts.net
Email: Hardworkingmail@hotmail.com
Twitter: @wooody3
FB and LinkedIn
(204) 955-0539

The Keystone Speakers is a Winnipeg, Manitoba, Canada-based group of speakers, facilitators, trainers, entertainers, technology, and management consultants. The organization formed with leaders in their respective fields banded together for mutual benefit.

A group of expert speakers in their respective fields came together in 2015 to form Keystone Speakers. Additionally, it has recruited exceptional outsiders to join in the journey to excellence in speaking and leadership and has become a leading group of experts.

Since inception, our members have spoken in ten countries on five continents. We deliver workshops, keynote speeches, seminars, consulting and coaching. The topics range from leadership, process improvement, business development and growth, self-esteem, and communication to professional and personal development.

This anthology is an excellent example of the expertise of our membership. The book was written with you in mind. It contains the cornerstones and keystones of business and personal success.

www.ingramcontent.com/pod-product-compliance
Lightning Source LLC
Chambersburg PA
CBHW070928160426
43193CB00011B/1608